Buen Camino!
Tips from an American Pilgrim

By Anne Born

Tumbleweed Pilgrim

Bronx, New York and Niles, Michiganñ

Tumbleweed Pilgrim

Dedicated to my first pilgrim companion,

my son, Charlie

Contents

I love my friends and family, but I also love it
when they can't find me and I can spend
all day reading or walking all alone, in silence,
eight thousand miles away from everyone.
All alone and unreachable in a foreign country
is one my most favorite possible things to be.

• Elizabeth Gilbert

Introduction

In 1971, I took an art history course at the University of Michigan called "Romanesque Sculpture of the Pilgrimage Road." The course was taught by an extraordinary medievalist named Ilene Forsyth. Focusing on northern Spanish medieval art, we also learned about her own analysis of the Romanesque sculptural program in the cloister at the monastery at Moissac in southwestern France. It was just a bonus. What I could not have known in 1971 was that Forsyth would spend the rest of her academic career exploring every square millimeter of that Moissac cloister.

She used a two-volume book written by Arthur Kingsley Porter as the basis for the course. As a young scholar in the 1920s, being aided by unlimited family funds, Porter sailed to Europe, hired a car and driver, and saw all of Europe as a destination the same way we might go just to Paris or Rome. And because of that broader view, he saw the *Camino de Santiago*, the centuries old pilgrimage road stretching across Spain, ending at the tomb of the Apostle James in Santiago de

1

Compostela, as if it were a thread tying many places together. Where his predecessors had routinely identified schools of art production based on place, like a "school" of Paris or a "school" of Rome, he saw that 11th and 12th century sculpture along the road to Santiago had similar characteristics and perhaps, sculptors and church builders were as itinerant as the pilgrims they served or the troubadours and poets who entertained them, after a hard day's work.

I was fascinated. As a young art historian myself, the idea that style could travel instead of remaining in one location was a game-changer in how I looked at and looked for the subtleties of any given piece of work. Porter believed that if troubadours and poets – and pilgrims – could travel easily and routinely from one place to the other along this road, maybe when the work was done at one church, sculptors and builders would do the same. This would account for the stylistic similarities he noticed along the *Camino*: everyone was walking with the pilgrims on their way to Santiago. They would build churches, finish their work, pack up, and move on to build another.

I kept this in the back of my mind for nearly four decades. Every time I would read something about the pilgrimage road, I would say to myself, "How wonderful to be able to see all those churches, strung like beads along the road to Santiago."

But I didn't go.

And it was simply because I had convinced myself that I needed three things to appear together in my life to be able to go: I needed the time, the money, and someone to travel with. If the three things didn't present themselves at the same time, along with my intermittent need to see medieval church sculptures, I figured I'd just wait. So, I waited. And I would read something, hear something about the *Camino* and repeat the mantra: "I must have three things." I'd have the money and no time to travel. Or I'd have the time and not the funds. And never once did I have anyone interested in coming along with me. Scaring up friends or family members to undertake a pilgrimage across Spain isn't as easy as it might sound.

Until 2009. That spring, I decided to press my then 18-year-old son into service and I took two weeks off work. The plan was to start in Paris, see how far we got, see what happened. I had read up a bit on what to bring, what to leave at home in order to be a successful pilgrim, but I also had decided this was to be more of a reconnaissance mission than anything serious like a full-on pilgrimage which, frankly speaking, terrified me even in 2009.

We flew to Paris, visited the Tour St. Jacques, the traditional starting point for pilgrims leaving Paris, and spent a few days shopping and seeing churches. Then, on to Toulouse, where I finally took a day trip out to Professor Forsyth's beloved cloister in the tiny town of Moissac. Just as I suspected, her sculpted cloister was glorious. My son read a bit under the sweeping pine tree I remembered from Professor Forsyth's projector slides so many years before, while I took pictures of the artwork.

Just a few days later, we took the train from Toulouse to St. Jean Pied de Port – the most popular starting point for the most popular route, the *Camino Francés*. We checked into the local pilgrims' office, spent the night in a lovely home, and set out to cross the Pyrenees at dawn the next day. A full twelve hours later, I dragged my sorry self into the town at the other side of the mountains where my son was resting comfortably at the bottom of a hill, waiting for me. We were in Spain, we had walked the first stage of the *Camino Francés*, we were in Roncesvalles. And I was sunburned, blistered, done.

I learned so many valuable lessons in one day of walking: I learned that I was still carrying way too much stuff. I learned that I would have to walk at my own pace and not try to keep up with an 18-year-old boy, and I learned that without sufficient motivation, no amount of planning or preparation would get me out the door again the next morning. We took a 45-minute cab ride to Pamplona, then a train to meet up with my daughter who lived in Madrid at the time.

But I was hooked. And I knew that now that I had acquired the serious motivation to walk again, I no longer needed anyone to come with me. All I needed was time – because, since I was working full-time, the funds were something I could deal with by putting some money aside, week by week.

The next year 2010 was a Holy Year, when the feast day of the Apostle Saint James falls on a Sunday and, in his honor, the Cathedral in Santiago opens their Holy Door to allow pilgrims to receive special blessings and to enter the church near the altar. I read an article in the *New York Times* that said they were getting ready to close the door on December 31 and that it would not be opened again until 2021. In that moment, I decided to go. I took two weeks' vacation and left on December 25, Christmas Day. My flight left only a few hours ahead of a devastating blizzard that would close all New York airports for days.

I flew to Madrid and took a bus to Sarria – the starting point of the last 100 kilometers of the *Camino Francés*. Pilgrims who start walking in Sarria, or at any point 100 kilometers out along one of the official routes, are eligible to receive the confirming document, the *Compostela*, saying they had completed the pilgrimage by walking the minimum allowable distance.

And I walked for five days, most of the way by myself. I stepped inside the Cathedral at 3:00 p.m. on New Year's Eve – only an hour and a half before they closed the door to get ready for the celebration that evening.

I had done it.

Since then, I have walked many segments of this pilgrimage road: in winter from León to Santiago de Compostela in 2012 with the eldest and youngest of my three daughters, I have walked during Advent from Roncesvalles – where I had left off with my son the year before — to Burgos with my middle daughter who then went on to walk to Santiago by herself, and in 2016, I picked up the trail again in Burgos in May and walked to León, again by myself. In July 2017, I walked another route coming down from the far north of Spain on the *Camino Primitivo*, starting in Oviedo and finishing again in Santiago. I work as a volunteer serving other pilgrims: once as a greeter in the Pilgrims' Office in Santiago and twice at The Abbey, just outside Pamplona. I've also worked in *albergues*, the designated pilgrims' hostels: in Ribadiso, Galicia just 40 or so kilometers outside of Santiago (twice!), and on the *Camino Primitivo* in Grado, Asturias. More recently, in April 2018, my friends and I walked the *Camino Inglés*, starting in Ferrol. I walked a gorgeous section of the *Camino Portugués* in April 2019 with my youngest daughter (a veteran pilgrim now), starting in Baiona. I say this a lot: I am always packed to walk the *Camino*.

And through it all, through all of these visits to Spain, I still wonder how it was that it took me so long to do this when, in 1971, I was so captivated by the *Camino*. I think I was more than likely just a product of that time. Most women I knew in 1971 did not feel empowered enough to take bold adventures, like hiking across Spain by themselves. And to be fair, the *Camino* was not nearly as popular then as it is now. I also wonder what my younger self would have made of it. I wonder too if I would have become the town crier for the *Camino* that I am now. I can tell you how frustrating it was walking from Sarria, finding that so many of the churches I had set out to see were not open when I walked by. I think that's ironic, and no, it did not stop me. I was walking in the footsteps of troubadours, poets, sculptors, architects, and yes, pilgrims.

So, I guess this is just the story of timid Anne from Niles, Michigan: a young girl who fell for the *Camino*, and the older lady who finally experienced it. It took me 38 years to get here. I would not like that to happen to you. If this interests you, please try it.

My hashtag these days is *#littleoldladywalking*. I'll post a glossary and some helpful resources and links to good websites, guidebooks, and movies about the *Camino*. And I've written you a personal letter, too – you'll see it at the end of the book.

Thank you to Stacey and Neil Quartaro for lending me the place I needed to finish this book, and my friends and family who read it: Johnnie Walker

Santiago, Mary Dorothy Baird, Ben Prusiner, Joan Haskins.

Thank you, Prof. Forsyth.

Buen Camino to all!

Some Basics

- The *Camino de Santiago* is a medieval pilgrimage route: a walk toward the Cathedral of Santiago de Compostela in northwestern Spain in the region of Galicia. The object is to visit the remains of the Apostle James the Greater which are housed in the Cathedral.

- There are many routes, many named *caminos* which start in several places in Spain, Portugal, Italy, and France and may include other locations in Europe feeding into the routes in Spain. The most famous – and by far the most popular – is the *Camino Francés*, beginning in southwest France in the small village of St. Jean Pied de Port.

- Pilgrims carry a scallop shell on their backpacks, the symbol of the pilgrim, along with an official pilgrim's passport, called a *credencial*. The *credencial* is stamped at designated pilgrim hostels (*albergues* in Spanish), shops, municipal offices, churches, bars, and restaurants to show where the pilgrim has stopped on their way to Santiago de Compostela. It is supplied by the Pilgrims' Office in Santiago de Compostela, or by writing to a recognized pilgrims' association such as the American Pilgrims on the Camino – or APOC as they are called – in the U.S. You will also find *credenciales* in Spanish church offices and *albergues*. You can find the shell at many souvenir shops.

o   Pilgrims greet each other with "*Bon Chemin!*" in France, and "*Buen Camino!*" when you arrive to start waking in Spain. It means, "Have a good walk, pilgrim." You'll hear that a lot. It's very encouraging and will most likely make you smile every time you hear it or say it.

o   Upon arriving in Santiago de Compostela, pilgrims present their *credencial* in the Pilgrims' Office and receive their completion document: the *Compostela*. This is the certificate that is awarded to pilgrims who have walked at minimum the last 100 kilometers. Pilgrims must be able to show they have walked that distance by the sequence of daily stamps on their *credencial.* (Just a note: it is possible also to bike, ride horseback or donkey, even wheelchair to qualify for the *Compostela*, but for this exercise, we'll just be discussing walking.)

o Once the pilgrimage is completed, pilgrims may also request a certificate of distance in the Pilgrims' Office, stating the starting point and the total number of kilometers covered. This document is popular both with pilgrims who have covered a significant distance walking to Santiago de Compostela and those of us who like the little extra nod for our accomplishment.

o Every day at noon, Catholic Mass is said for arriving pilgrims in the Cathedral of Santiago de Compostela. The nationality and the point where the days' arriving pilgrims started walking is read during the service: "Starting in Burgos, pilgrims from the United States." One of the signature parts of the pilgrim Mass is the *botafumeiro* –

the 80 kg, 1,60 meters high incense burner that is swung at the close of the Mass by a team of maroon-robed men (*tiraboleiros* in Spanish). These *tiraboleiros* will swing the *botafumeiro* across the transept, the crossing arm of the Cathedral, up to the ceiling of the church. It is not presented at every Mass, but if you are fortunate enough to see it, you will probably carry the image with you for a long, long while. Mass is also offered regularly in the Cathedral in English. The best view is from the transept.

Please note that while the Cathedral is under renovations (2019-2020), Masses have been moved out of the building to other churches nearby and the *botafumeiro* is temporarily out of commission. Look for both to return to celebrate the next Holy Year, which will open on December 31, 2020. In the meanwhile, you will still be able to visit the crypt and embrace the Apostle. Just check the board at the entrance for operating hours. There is no fee to enter this church.

What is a Pilgrimage?

This is a fundamental discussion, important to planning as well as execution.

It's easy when you are shopping for boots, looking at maps, picking which route, which days, which month you want to walk, to lose sight of why we walk this route. This is a walk in a sacred space where pilgrims for hundreds of years have left their footprints only to have them covered by the footprints of the pilgrims who follow. The *Camino* is a space filled with the prayers and cares of so many people. If you keep that in mind, you should find this is one of the most challenging and fulfilling events of your life.

But walking to Santiago is not just for Catholics or the extremely religious and saintly. While it's necessary to say here that this route will take you to a Catholic church to be in the presence of the remains of a martyr who followed Jesus' admonition to "Preach to the ends of the earth," the journey is something from which everyone can learn. Arriving at the crypt, kneeling in that small room; this can be overwhelming to

17

someone who is very religious. To someone else, it can be a moment of complete spiritual clarity. And to an exhausted pilgrim, it can be a very emotional moment.

While each pilgrim will have to view their gains or losses personally, it is safe to say that the days of walking – of solitude, of camaraderie, of asking for help or aiding your colleagues – that will be the real benefit and that benefit is not confined to or experienced by one religious group or people. It may not be something that makes you feel in any way closer to God. Maybe you will feel closer to a real understanding of yourself. At the most basic part of it, however, it is a sublime human endeavor and its simplicity can be liberating.

Why Do People Go on a Pilgrimage?

Why do people do this? What makes people want to walk for miles and miles across Spain just to pray in an old church?

I have some experience listening to pilgrims tell why they do this. When I worked as an Amigo volunteer in the Pilgrims' Office in Santiago de Compostela, I listened to pilgrims' stories every day that ranged from simple, "I am doing this in thanksgiving for my life!" to the heartbreaking, "My husband died while we were walking last year and I am finishing our pilgrimage now for him," to the profound, "Our dad died while getting ready to walk and we decided to come together as brothers to walk in his memory."

Some are grateful they are cancer-free. Some tell about being in Europe for other reasons or hearing about the *Camino* from friends. I met a man while volunteering at The Abbey, a former fortress-church that has recently been purchased by my friends. A man came by who had just come to Spain from France where he met the son of the man who had rescued his dad during WWII when his dad's plane crashed at sea. Without the help of the man's father, this pilgrim's dad would not have survived. His pilgrimage? The perfect segue from that emotional experience.

I met two girls, one from the U.S., one from Canada, who were studying abroad in Logroño and after seeing pilgrims walking there, wanted to know what it was like to become pilgrims. We stopped together in Najera overnight where the *hospitalero* – a volunteer looking after the pilgrims who spend the night in one of the pilgrim hostels – joked that "Americans" never bring sleeping bags! But they were just walking a few days and had next to no planning or preparation. They just had a few days off.

I can tell you about the pilgrims I met from the Netherlands or France, or South America, Italy, Austria, South Africa. Or the group of four Spanish married couples who had been walking together over the past four years, bit by bit, stage by stage, over long holiday weekends and vacations. I met them when they arrived at the Pilgrims' Office in Santiago. They were still together and jubilant at having finished, after walking for so long. I would guess they did this to be able to spend more time together.

An older man walked the 12 or so kilometers just from Logroño to Navarrete with my daughter and me. His wife had driven ahead to meet him for lunch in the next town. He just needed the time to walk.

What you will find is that it is the people you remember more than anything else: I met a group of young men, lifelong friends who set out from their homes together in Oviedo, and three priests walking together from their home in Poland, one of whom danced his way down the hill in the morning. Or the two young men from South Korea who stopped to volunteer at The Abbey, the newlyweds, two newly-engaged pilgrims, and one couple, planning to walk on past Santiago to the water's edge in Finisterre to be married at the end of their *Camino*, with friends and their families waiting there to celebrate their marriage.

As a pilgrim, sometimes you know why you're doing this. Sometimes you find out why. All the time though, the walking will speak to you in a very personal way. Many pilgrims will never talk about why they are walking, while others are happy to share.

There's a Latin expression that is quite popular among pilgrims: *solvitur ambulando.* In one sense it is meant to focus on the benefits of taking a walk. "It is solved by walking." It has another meaning and I think they both apply to this pilgrimage walk. "It is solved bit by bit by slowly moving ahead," as if walking toward a goal.

So, what is the *Camino de Santiago* anyway? What is it supposed to do? Is it a vacation, a long hike, a road trip to Spain? Is it a chance to rediscover yourself, a way to fill a hiatus between jobs or lovers? A reward, or conversely, an elaborate way of repaying a debt? How about a way to meet new people or spend some time by yourself?

There is no single right way or wrong way to execute a successful pilgrimage. You'll have the chance to learn something. Something real.

We live our lives indoors, for the most part; sitting at desks, phoning in lunch, taking trains or buses, driving our cars, running errands, having groceries delivered. But what if you could walk away from that predictable life and rely on your skills, your instincts for even a day? Wouldn't that change the way you looked at your routine? What if you could only have with you a single change of clothes and a second pair of shoes? Wouldn't that change the way you looked at your "stuff?" All that stuff we surround ourselves with will seem so superfluous after spending a week or longer where, as pilgrims, we concentrate on walking the road ahead, not worried about much more than where we will spend the night.

When I came home from my last walk, I set down my backpack, changed my clothes, and picked up my regular day bag – the one I carry to and from work every day in New York. It weighed nearly the same as the pack I had carried with my clothes, a quilt, my water bottle, bathroom items, and passport. What was I doing dragging all that stuff with me every day? Why did I need all the stuff? Was that what I was supposed to learn?

There are countless discussions of whether it is the journey or the destination that should motivate you to walk one of the medieval paths to the Cathedral – and there are many routes to take. For some, the very act of walking 20 kilometers or more each day over time, as most pilgrims do, will be prayerful enough. For others, it becomes a race to see how far you can go each day in order to speed toward the destination.

I guess if I had all the time in the world and all the money in the world, I would walk only about 15 kilometers or so every day, in order to be able to savor each town, each region, each day – with time left over to write! But, in fact, I have found that I am always so happy to arrive at the Cathedral that on my walk in 2017, I covered a day and a half's worth of walking in one day to be in Santiago in time for evening Mass.

Pilgrimage. It will also bestow an unexpected level of anonymity to you. As you walk, as you eat in bars and restaurants, stay in hostels, talk with other pilgrims, you can be known as Grace from New York or Ben from California. Nothing more than that. No long histories, no family baggage, no lengthy explanations or work worries – you are simply a pilgrim, one equal to the next. I realized this in 2010 when I stopped to ask a bartender to call me a cab so I could go off the road for a short while to visit a Templar chapel. He said on the phone, "I have a pilgrim here who would like to see the church." In that moment, I realized I had become a pilgrim. That was powerful stuff. He didn't know who I was or why it was important to me to visit that chapel. He saw a pilgrim needing a ride.

In fact, I have come to understand that the pilgrimage begins not when you arrive at your starting point in Europe, but when you make the decision to go. Planning, picking out gear, reading through guidebooks and maps – all of this will be done as a pilgrim, not as a civilian planning to become a pilgrim. The path will carry you, and the path will sustain you – if you let it.

I'm going to make suggestions – which you may follow or not – that are based on my walking the *Camino*

Francés, the *Camino Primitivo*, and the *Camino Inglés* in sections over time. Everyone plots out their own route to the Apostle. Mine tends to tumble across Spain rather than follow a single, recognizable path.

So, is it the journey or the destination? It's both really. Walking 20 plus kilometers each day over days or weeks on end just to get a piece of paper will probably leave you unsatisfied. But walking each day to learn more about your fellow pilgrims, to visit small churches and holy sites, to spend time alone with your thoughts, and to find yourself, at the end of the journey, in the crypt of the cathedral, praying in gratitude for your family and your loved ones — that can be enormously rewarding. That's why I do it.

Do you need to believe – in anything? What you think you believe in at the start will be challenged at every step. Are the saint's remains really there? Saint James died in Jerusalem and his remains were transported to Spain by a miracle. Do you believe in the miracles that are the basis for most pilgrimages; to Lourdes, Fatima, Bethlehem? Does it matter if you find yourself questioning everything you believe in? No. That's what this is about.

Pilgrims on the *Camino de Santiago* set out to do one thing: just to walk. You walk from one place to the next until you arrive at the destination: the beautiful cathedral with the small silver casket. Simple.

What Is a Typical Day for a Pilgrim?

Pilgrims get up early to get walking as the sun comes up. Some pilgrims like to leave before daylight but if you are planning to do this, make sure you have the following in place: check to see when the *albergue* opens in the morning because some are locked overnight, make sure you know where you're going, hold your cellphone in your hand as you exit the building, and be sure you carry sufficient light. It's wonderful to watch the sun rise behind you in the morning.

Breakfast may be available at your *albergue* or at a local bar. Make sure you have a filled water bottle before leaving. Be sure to use the *fuentes,* too. These are small roadside fountains where you should just empty out what water you have in your water bottle and refill it with fresh, cold water from the fountain. The ones for drinking are marked either *fuentes* or *potable* and are on most maps. The ones NOT for drinking will be marked *NO Potable.* Pay attention – and make sure the spigot works <u>before</u> emptying out your water!

And then you walk. Using an app on your phone – or two! – and paper maps or guidebooks. As a personal choice, I much prefer apps and have not walked using any paper maps yet, other than in planning.

When you start walking, you will also start looking for arrows. You won't lose your way if you pay attention and follow them — and thank Don Elías, a priest from O'Cebreiro who had the idea in the early 1970s to mark the *Camino* with painted yellow arrows.

There are arrows painted on streets, on poles, on trees, on bridges, and on stone way-markers to keep you on the route. You get used to looking for them and they tend to appear when you need reassurance that you didn't take a wrong turn. But if you walk a bit and do not see them, don't be afraid to retrace your steps to make sure you are still on the road. The arrows are key and the single most important part of your getting where you need to be on any given day. If you do get lost or miss a turn, don't be afraid to ask someone where the road goes – they'll probably know and, in many cases, will walk a bit with you to make sure you're OK.

I once walked up to the foot of a mountain on somebody's farm after I missed one arrow that would have led me down the hill. The farmer's little girl spotted me and ran to get her dad who looked at me incredulously: "You missed the arrow! It's on the third house on the right. *Buen Camino!*" They waved. I waved.

In addition to the arrows, there are shells. Sometimes you will see them in the pavement in the larger cities like Pamplona and Lugo, and sometimes they will be on ceramic plaques embedded into the stone way markers. It's not always clear which way they are pointing, because typically the image of the shell is laid on its side, either with the base of the shell to the right or to the left. This directional signal changes from region to region in Spain, so while it's lovely to see them, it's always going to be better if you stick with the arrows.

Mid-day, after walking for several hours, it pays to find your way to a bar or a place to take a short break and get something to eat, to drink, and a stamp for your *credencial*. It's remarkable how refreshing it can be to get a few minutes' rest and a drink of something cold after walking for three to four hours, and most bars leave their stamp for your *credencial* right on the bar.

Arriving at the day's stopping point, you will check in, shower, wash whatever clothes need washing, and get some rest. Maybe you rest drinking a cold beer at the local bar with some of the pilgrims you've been walking with, maybe over prayers in the church, maybe lying on your bunk staring at your feet (my personal favorite) – but it's so important to look after yourself and to get the rest you need.

Then, you get a nice dinner, explore your surroundings, or spend some time lying down. Some pilgrims like to shop for food and cook if there is a kitchen where you are staying and it is available for pilgrims to use. Always check with the staff before shopping for food, because even if there is a kitchen, it's not always open to pilgrims. I much prefer to eat at the local bars and restaurants. I'm not much of a cook and I love to talk to the wait staff about their town and their impression of passing pilgrims.

"Lights out" is typically at 10:00 p.m., if you are staying at an *albergue*. Please remember to bring ear plugs (to block the snoring!) and keep a little flashlight next to you. Pretty much everybody snores on some level and the flashlight can help get you to the bathroom safely in the middle of the night or if you get up before "Lights On" in the morning.

Albergues typically will have blankets for pilgrims to use: some charge a few euros, some are free to use. It can be seriously cold, if you are up in the mountains in Spain – even in July and August. And yes, there are mountains.

A footnote on how to "claim" your bed in an albergue: while you must not put your backpack on the bunks, please be sure to leave something on the bed to say, "I've landed. This territory is mine tonight." Leave your bathroom items, leave your sleeping bag, leave a water bottle. Otherwise, somebody can plop on down and you'll find yourself left with a bunk on the top by the door – most people's least favorite place to sleep. Many albergues leave the best bed to the last arriving pilgrim, but it's just a better strategy to take a bed when you arrive, plant a proverbial flag, and go out and get that nice dinner.

What Do I Need?

It used to be that you needed a note from your parish priest in the U.S. to qualify as a bonafide pilgrim. I do ask my priest for a blessing before I leave each time. I figure it can't hurt, right?

So, take the blessing, and add ultra-lightweight hiking gear: great, waterproof hiking boots or shoes, a backpack, a change of clothes, a serious rain cover, and my one essential – especially recommended for pilgrims not accustomed to long days of continuous hiking – hiking poles.

Why ultra-lightweight? Carry five pounds of flour up a flight of stairs. Now, pick up another sack and carry ten pounds of flour up a flight of stairs. If you notice a difference, imagine carrying that same 10 pounds for days and you'll see why the weight of the things you carry becomes a serious consideration. You will want to choose light clothes, small travel-sized versions of your bathroom items, and a light quick dry towel. Ultimately, other than a second pair of comfortable lightweight shoes, you probably won't need more than a second set of clothes and something light to sleep in. When you are finished packing, you will want to assess the weight of the pack – keeping the overall weight to not more than 10% of your body weight (you weigh 150 pounds, you carry no more than 15 pounds). Or less! A full water bottle will add another 2 pounds. Camera? Look for a tiny one that fits in your pocket.

One of the best components of this type of trip is you don't spend more than one night in each place; meaning if you walk the entire *Camino Francés*, you will have spent the night in nearly three dozen different locations. This also means, unlike spending many nights in the same place like we do on vacations, you have to get used to where everything is every night before you go to sleep. That pocket flashlight will come in handy.

If you are used to traveling with binoculars, hair dryers, computers, games, or other gear, please leave it all at home. A pilgrimage should not be a working vacation and, seriously, nobody will care if your hair looks amazing. To save weight, I will leave my house keys at home.

While it's tempting to be cavalier about what you can carry and how much you will need your stuff, I have seen what happens to pilgrims whose packs are too big and too heavy. I greeted a family of four this past July; two teenage children and their parents. They each carried backpacks the length of their torso plus about a foot in height over that. By the time they had arrived at the *albergue*, it was way past dinner time when most pilgrims arrive in the early to mid-afternoon, and they were exhausted. The extra weight will impact your stamina certainly, but it will also impact your knees, it can affect your balance, and it can turn what should be an enjoyable time of quiet reflection into a real hardship.

Let's talk gear.

Shoes – there are lots of ways to look at this item. Your shoes will become your friend or your foe depending on how you buy them and ultimately, how you wear them. I recommend lightweight waterproof hiking boots. I need the extra ankle support from higher boots and have found that it's not always the boots that need breaking in, it's the socks.

When I bought my first boots years ago, I listened to the lady in the store who told me I absolutely had to have heavy wool blend hiking socks and that the real serious hikers all wore them. Perhaps that is the case. But I wore my boots to work every day for a week before I left and found that the wool socks made my feet too hot and cramped my toes. I swapped them out for some "6 Pairs for $5" socks from the discount place and I was happy. In the beginning I got a few minor blisters, but I was so much better off. And I wouldn't have known this if I hadn't worked so hard to break in the boots!

Spend some serious time trying them on when you shop. A great pair will cry out to you, "These are your boots!" I know my last pair did. Keep in mind too that they do not last forever. Just like running shoes that start to break down after so many miles traveled, so do boots. If you have some, and you've worn them a while, consider buying new ones. They will fit better right out of the box than boots from years ago, but you still need to get them used to your feet! And don't forget to break in your socks, too.

Now you've got socks and lightweight waterproof boots. Time to add the poles.

There are lots of folks who do not use hiking poles and even more who will argue loudly against them. However, I believe that this is where to spend the money. Get lightweight collapsible poles and you will have something to catch you if you start to fall, keep you balanced along uneven trails, and sweep away the ferns and bushes that crowd the trails in many places. They displace your weight and can make walking easier. You will get used to the tapping sound they make. There's nothing better for going downhill over rocks or slate.

And the backpack – I keep the weight of my empty backpack under two pounds so that I can fill it and not go above 14 pounds – my top weight for carrying something on my back. Many light packs will also have support pieces you can remove to make them even lighter, but try it out, fill it up, make sure it's something you can carry without issue. I like to say, if you keep thinking about your backpack, it might not be the right one for you. Backpacks come in sizes, they come in men's and women's models, and many manufacturers have YouTube videos showing the key components and features.

What features do you absolutely need? It is helpful not to have to take off your backpack simply to get a drink of water from your water bottle. You might look for large side pockets that you can reach. Remember though, the more features, the more weight; you don't need lots of extra carrying-handles or zippers or compartments that have extra pockets – seriously, everything weighs something.

Keep the pack simple. It does not have to be waterproof – most packs even now are not waterproof – and you probably don't need a waterproof cover. The flaw in these covers is they do not cover the straps. And once the straps are saturated with water, they will make everything wet on either side of them. Consider lining your pack with a 13-gallon plastic kitchen trash bag. It's a very simple fix.

How do you keep *you* from getting wet? Lots of pilgrims pack stadium rain ponchos but I think they are pretty unwieldy if it's also windy. I invested in a light rain poncho with a terrific special feature – it fits over me and my backpack. All snug and dry. You can find these in lots of places, if you look for hiking ponchos.

Now you have boots, poles, and the pack. And you're ready for the rain in Spain! Don't believe that it stays mainly on the plain. It's pretty much everywhere. But then, you aren't traveling here for the weather, are you?

Are you ready to assemble your little items?

Pack a quick dry towel. Buy the biggest one you can find. It will save you on several levels, not just drying you after your shower. If you walk in the summer and can hang your wet, washed things outdoors, your clothes should dry overnight. But if it rains overnight, you might wake up to soggy duds. Not a great way to start your day. That is where that quick dry towel can help. You roll up your clothes in the towel and transfer the moisture to something that dries more quickly.

I once had an *hospitalera* offer to "wash" my clothes for me which I thought meant "dry" as well. It did not. So, after dinner, I found my soggy duds in a plastic bin where I was supposed to gather them up and hang them outdoors on the line in the courtyard. But I couldn't get outdoors because the *albergue* was locked by the time I found them. We live, we learn, right? Don't expect anyone to be responsible for your having dry, clean clothes but you.

Sleeping bag? Necessary or just one more thing? Since I like to walk in the winter, I believed a sleeping bag was the one thing I did need. I could leave a lot behind but my sleeping bag was essential. But it weighed nearly two pounds and it was bulky. So, I swapped it out for a lightweight, just-as-warm, down travel blanket that weighs 8 ounces less than the bag and folds up smaller. And I was just as happy, just as warm. I did not sleep all zipped up anyway and tended to use my sleeping bag as a blanket. Again, your overnight temperature level, either warm or cool, is your responsibility.

Look for lightweight clothes, too. There are a number of places to get long pants and moisture-wicking shirts that weigh next to nothing. This is not a license to over pack simply because you've got lightweight stuff! Rather it's a way to make sure you have what you need. Start with two pairs of socks, underwear, one pair of pants, one short sleeve shirt, one long sleeve shirt. This is a year 'round solution. And leave blue jeans at home. Then add another pair of pants and a sweater of some sort. I like cashmere because it's very light and extremely warm for the weight, but there are a number of fun lightweight jackets. If you are walking in winter, try a "three-in-one" jacket – a waterproof outer shell and a long sleeve fleece or down jacket to wear underneath. You can use both pieces during the day and still have a light jacket to wear indoors at night. Many places do not have heat or they limit the heat because paying for heat in Spain is so very expensive. If it's 55 degrees outside, it could very well be 55 degrees inside. You'll be glad you have that fleece.

You will also need some "evening" shoes. Not fancy satin pumps but rather something light so you can give your feet a rest from your boots. I like slip-ons, something with the new memory-foam soles. My feet like them, too! Many pilgrims carry flip-flops for shower use. I'm not a flip-flop fan, but I do see the benefit of keeping your feet off a wet, common shower floor.

How about a hat? I have to be honest: I am just not a hat guy. I have worn three different hats while walking in Spain, but they all had different outcomes. The first was a slimmed down Merino wool watch cap that I used for a few days while walking in December. The next was a floppy Aussie hat that looked very legit and made me feel like I was an international travel expert, fresh off safari. It lasted one morning because when I looked up while wearing it, all I could see was the brim when all I wanted to see was the sky. The last hat met with much greater success. I realized my little baseball cap would keep the sun off my face. I wore it over many days and would recommend wearing a baseball cap to anyone who thinks a hat would help.

Bathroom items come in travel sizes. I have found that one tiny travel toothpaste tube and shampoo bottle will last about a week, using it sparingly. If you run out of something like this, you may not find small, travel-sized ones to replace it, so bring two or three and toss them when they're done. Chapstick has many uses beyond lip balm. I use it on blisters to help repair the skin and it's great for small cuts, chapped cuticles – and chapped lips. Dental floss is also handy for other uses.

Travel size is the only way to go. Heavy full-size bottles are never going to be an asset to your walk.

Will you need moisturizer, lipstick, mascara, makeup? Probably not. A brush AND a comb? Maybe not. Conditioner, body wash, shaving cream – all of these items weigh something. Try to see how few topics there are that you must cover – if you save a few ounces here and a few there, you may find your pack is a pound lighter. That's huge in this business.

Fog, light, reflector strips: not all walking is in forests or farmland. You will find yourself walking in, on, and near highways sometimes and if you are walking really early, approaching twilight, or in the fog, you will be glad that you added reflector strips to your pack or your wardrobe.

I have a great bright yellow Buff with silver reflector strips. Buffs are quite popular with pilgrims because you can use them to keep your neck warm or hold your hair out of your face. In many ways these tubes of stretchy fabric will act like bandannas with the added benefit that you are less likely to lose them because they don't need to be tied to keep them on you.

Weigh everything – both in the practical sense and in the grander metaphysical sense. Consider leaving things at home that you normally cannot live without. This is the nature of pilgrimage. You step away from your routine, you leave your home, your comforts, your family, your friends, and your things – all in the hope of being able to spend time alone, to be able to pray, to be open to the road ahead of you, and to concentrate on the simplest of activities: walking. Things weigh something.

In the classic *Camino* book, "To Walk Far, Carry Less," the author, Jean-Christie Ashmore, recounts a conversation he had with a Spanish pilgrim. Jean-Christie had packed too much and was feeling it after just two days walking. The Spanish pilgrim told him, "We carry our fears in our backpack."

Consider this one carefully: we carry a sweater because we are afraid it could be cold. We carry a rain coat because we are afraid it could rain, Kleenex because we are afraid we could catch cold, and on and on. "I might need this, this would be good to have just in case, what if something happens, what if I can't find this at the pharmacy?" Or, "I'm certain I'll need this in case something happens."

Strip down to the necessary and leave these fears behind. You aren't leaving the galaxy. You are just going to Spain.

What else do you need to bring?

A rock.

Seriously. You need to carry a small rock in your pocket to leave along the road. If you walk the *Camino Francés* and start east of or at Foncebadón, you will take it to the *Cruz de Ferro* and leave it with everyone else's little rock. The rock is meant to symbolize the burdens you carry – and symbolically, you will leave them here.

The *Cruz de Ferro* is just that – a tall iron cross on top of a mound of little rocks. It might not sound impressive now, but trust me, when you get there, it will be one of the moments you remember.

All along the road, on the other *caminos* and on the rest of the *Camino Francés*, you will find rocks left by pilgrims. Sometimes they are left after a short prayer of gratitude that the burden is lifted, sometimes they are just deposited there on top of a way marker, memorialized in a cellphone photo, and left to inspire pilgrims who follow.

And bring freezer style Zip-Locs.

A rock for your soul, Zip-Locs for your stuff. I bring two gallon-sized freezer Zip-Locs for my clothes. On one bag, I write "DIRTY" and on the other, wait for it…, I write "CLEAN." This is because, after a few days, none of your clothes will look all that clean at first glance. When you check in for the night, regardless of where you stay, you will want to wash your dirty clothes right away so they have the best chance to dry before you take off in the morning. So, if you take a shower, you just add the clothes you were wearing to the "DIRTY" bag and you are ready to do the wash. It's a simple trick that helps me a lot.

You will do a fair amount of hand washing of your clothes, but more and more *albergues* are offering not only soap for you to use, but washing machines or washing services to their visiting pilgrims.

Why freezer Zip-Locs? The regular baggies tend to break down if you use them again and again, so I like the heavier freezer ones. But keep in mind, plastic bags will make an awful noise. The worst are the ones you pick up at fruit markets and smaller shops. Be sure to keep this in mind as you settle into your bunk for the night. Make sure all of your plastic bags are safely stowed before "Lights Out." And do not go through them in the morning. Get out of the dormitory and then go through your pack. Your fellow pilgrims will love you for that.

I was assigned a bed in a small dormitory on the *Camino Primitivo* last July with two other pilgrims. Four beds, three occupants. I had planned to get up at 6:00 a.m., but one of the other pilgrims decided 5:00 a.m. was a far better choice. So he set an alarm that sounded like it was summoning the local volunteer fire brigade and it took him about a minute to turn it off. Now I'm awake and I'm not happy. Unbeknownst to me, the night before, he had distributed all of his little items all around the room. I listened to Velcro, snaps, zippers, and easily a dozen crinkly plastic bags as they went from his hands to his pack, then back out of his pack, then back into the pack. I said, "Steve? What are you doing? Can you go outdoors to do this?" He said, "No, there's no place outside. I have to pack here." I said, "Steve. The whole planet is outside this room."

Don't be like Steve. Be considerate and pack up everything the night before, set your alarm to vibrate or the sound of crickets, and then slip right outside and leave your fellow pilgrims to sleep.

And bring your phone! I know people who will shout, "Just unplug! Go off the grid! Leave your phone at home." But I keep my phone handy for two reasons: I can check in with my family so they know where I am, and I take lots of pictures so my Facebook family knows where I am. In the event you do need to make an emergency call, either to aid yourself or to help another pilgrim, you will be so glad you have it.

I like to get my family to download the *Camino* guide I decide to use. That way, when I say, "I made it to Hornillos!" they know what I mean and where I am simply by opening the app.

And download the Kindle app for your phone. You can store lots of books there and the John Brierley *Camino Francés* guide – easily the single most popular English language guidebook to the *Camino* – has a Kindle version with maps of the stages. It's great not to carry paper books but still to have the option of reading them. When I walked with my two daughters in 2012, we read the classic story of pilgrimage, "The Canterbury Tales," to each other at night.

When Do I Go?

Most pilgrims walk over vacations, summer break from school, long weekends, and during retirement. Since the walk can take some time, depending on how you plan, my recommendation is to find the most convenient time for you and start laying out a route. Routes are divided into a typical day's walking: 20 kilometers or so as a standard, going up to 30 or so. These divisions are referred to commonly as stages. There is no absolute requirement to stick to walking these stages as they are presented in the standard guidebooks unless they suit your own needs. By staying off-stage or mid-stage, you can visit smaller, less crowded towns and villages. I've done both and much prefer not to stay at the end of a published, identified stage. I'll either keep walking a bit or stop a bit short of the day's end.

If you select the *Camino Francés* and plan to walk it from the traditional starting point in the French Pyrenees, your pilgrimage will take a little over a month to complete, depending on how far you walk each day and how many days you take off to rest. Or you could choose to start walking in Sarria instead of St. Jean, and the walk would take you five or six days. In each case, you would qualify for the *Compostela* – assuming you walk the entire 100 last kilometers to reach Santiago.

If you fly from the U.S., you would arrive in Spain sometime the next day, use the day to get to your starting point, spend that night there, and walk the following morning. This means, simply, that if you leave on Monday, your first day walking would be Wednesday. It's fairly easy to get to any of the bigger towns along the *Camino Francés* by bus (ALSA line and others) or train (Renfe and others) from Madrid or Barcelona if you think you'd like to start walking from Pamplona or Burgos, for instance. To plan your route to the starting point of your walk, use Rome2rio. It's a website and an invaluable app.

The months of January to April are the least traveled months for pilgrims. If you are motivated by a need for serious "alone" time, this would be ideal. The weather can be downright nasty with cold rain or snow in many locations, but the payoff can be that you have the better part of the day to walk by yourself.

If you are looking for company and look forward to meeting other pilgrims from all over the world and getting to know them, you might want to walk between May and October. The plus side is that you will actually meet pilgrims everywhere you go along the *Camino*, but the minus could be that you find yourself in crowded accommodations with noise and distractions, and that time away you had planned for quiet reflection is not possible in the way you planned.

November and December are my favorite months to walk. I love the shorter days, the quiet, the season of Advent, and the different way people will look after you when you are not part of a crowd. It's a lovely, lonely time to be a pilgrim and the atmosphere is so different from what I suppose you could call "high season." Winter pilgrims do need a heightened awareness of both less available daylight to walk in during the shorter days, and fewer available resources, because much of the pilgrim infrastructure will close for the season.

There is a kind of network of overnight accommodations – they all know who's open, who's closed or about to close, and the staff will gladly give you directions forward so you know where to stay. In any season. You can walk into any open *albergue* and ask for help of any kind – Band-Aids, medical assistance, water, a place to rest for a moment, a cup of tea or some cookies, or a phone to make a local call if you need someone to help you with it. They are there to aid pilgrims in their walk and will have someone on site who either speaks English or knows someone who does.

Where Do Pilgrims Stay?

In many cases, pilgrims spend the night in *albergues*, frequently staffed by volunteers. An *albergue* is a designated pilgrim hostel, typically with a large dormitory room or rooms filled with bunk beds. As you reach your stopping point for the day and arrive at an *albergue*, you will be greeted by an *hospitalero* who will take your country passport and your *credencial* and check you in for the night. *Hospitaleros* look after pilgrims and collect data on the number of people who spend the night, their citizenship, and the place where they began walking. In most *albergues*, you will only be able to spend one night.

There are private *albergues* that will take reservations for a bed over the phone or online, and there are municipal *albergues* that will only accept pilgrims as they appear at their door. Lists of all available options are found online in several places, depending on the *Camino* you are walking. In some stops, depending on the size of the town, there can be small local hotels called *pensiónes* in Spanish, and in the large cities like

Pamplona, Logroño, Burgos, León, there are also larger, more luxurious accommodations. A night in a *pensión* might just be the relaxing stay that you need after several nights in *albergues*. They are small, family-run, low to no frills hotels with few to no amenities other than a clean private room and bath. I love to mix it up and try a variety of places to stay.

The classic *albergue* is what is called a *donativo* – you may pay what you wish, but you do need to pay something and the amount is up to you. To me, the most satisfying overnight experience anywhere is at a *donativo*. I've had gourmet meals with printed menus, I've had my clothes washed and dried and delivered to me folded, I've had the *hospitalero* wake us up with soft, classical music and pots of hot coffee. In other words, do not think that just because the place is "by donation" and not at a fixed rate charge, it's not a lovely, clean, friendly, and well-staffed place.

There's a story in every *albergue*: the man who checked me into an *albergue* on the *Camino Primitivo*, saying, "We are a family here. No alarms. We will decide as a family when to wake up." Or the man who was volunteering at a place on the *Camino Francés* whose daughter studied Flamenco dancing. She and my daughter danced together to entertain the pilgrims. Or the *hospitalero* near the *Cruz de Ferro* who took me outside when I came down for breakfast on Christmas Day, showing me that it had snowed the night before and we would have a white Christmas.

I checked into an *albergue* in Castrojeríz ahead of a man who had been walking with me all morning. As he reaches for his wallet, he realizes he left it at the bar back along the road, roughly an hour back – cash, credit cards, and his passport. The *hospitalero* said, "Please don't worry, I'll help you." He called the bar, spoke with the barman who had found the wallet, and then drove back with my friend to pick it up.

As much as I will defend anyone's decision to stay in hotels, as I have done so frequently, I will also recommend you do not miss staying in any one of these dozens of unique and remarkable places to stay.

I've only stayed at one *casa rural*, but that was an amazing experience and I would recommend it. I definitely would stay there again. A wonderful guest house out in the middle of nowhere, right on the *Camino Primitivo*, I found this antique stone complex that offered plush accommodations, gourmet food, and a lovely terrace where I could write in my little journal about what I had for breakfast and lunch the day before. And to get in, I just walked by and knocked on the door. Most people will book ahead at a *casa rural*, I just got lucky.

The common denominator in every one of these options is this: as a walking pilgrim, you will be looked after, cared for, and protected. The places you stay have housed pilgrims for years. Please remember this when you check in: you are a tiny part of a much greater, ongoing activity that began over a thousand years ago. On any given day, someone is walking toward Santiago de Compostela, aided by the kind people along the route.

Here is my request: if the staff of the *albergue* says that the kitchen closes at 9:30 p.m., don't be the guy who lingers in the kitchen making it impossible for the staff to clean up for the night. If the staff says they close and lock the front door at 10:00 p.m. to keep pilgrims safe, don't be the guy who sits at the café down the hill until they close at 2:00 a.m. expecting someone to let you in. And if you find that you can only do hand washing of your clothes, don't whine that the last place did your laundry for you. Be gracious. Most of the staff will be former pilgrims. Be the guy they would like to house again. Help clean up, help wash dishes, help sweep the floor – but always ask first.

The other question *you* will have to answer is this: will you be comfortable and happy finding your daily accommodations on the fly or will you need to have a plan to stick to that includes lots and lots of reservations? This is a tough one. The issues concerning where you will spend the night every night are not insurmountable and, in fact, it can be the most memorable part of your walk.

I've walked off-season, off-stage, alone, with no reservations. I suppose that's the extreme, but it created the pilgrimage experience I wanted at the time and I would do it again. I let the road rise up to meet me, as my Irish ancestors might have said. I stayed at *albergues* and *pensiónes* and found a nice, sometimes warm place every night for weeks – without needing the security of having a reservation and a guarantee of a bed. Only once did I have to walk on to the next town to find a place to spend the night.

For so many reasons, I think this is how you learn the most about the *Camino*. When it looks like everything is either closed or full, someone will scoop you up and give you a place to stay. I've stayed in otherwise empty *pensiónes* and *albergues*. I've gotten the last bed in places, the first in others. I've had hotel desk clerks take one look at me, dragging in after a long day's walk, and say, "Here's your room key, *señora*. Go upstairs and lie down or get a shower, and come back to me later to check in." And once, my daughters and I found the *albergue* was closed but there was a note and a phone number to call if we needed a place and we were given keys to a house with a stocked kitchen, WiFi, and a fireplace.

I walked in the pouring rain all afternoon with my daughters once. When we arrived in the town where we wanted to spend the night, I asked the bartender at the first bar that was open, where we might find a place to stay. He picked up the phone and called his friend who owned the *pensión* across the street. His friend came running toward us, apologizing it took him five minutes to get to us. He then opened his *pensión* to us, gathered up our dirty clothes and put them in the wash, recommending we go downstairs to his friend's restaurant to get dinner while our clothes were washing. When we got back after dinner, he was taking our things out of the drier and making sure we had the WiFi password before he left for the night. We had an entire building to ourselves.

Where you spend the night will teach you so much about this walk. Typically, when you check into a hotel on vacation, you will never speak to the other guests. But when you stay in an *albergue*, odds are you will be sleeping three feet from another "guest" or 20 other guests, and they all probably helped cook dinner. They quickly become your family and you know them as "Adriana from San Antonio," "Nina from New York," "John from Scotland," or "Stephanie from Kansas City," "Stacey from Toronto."

Pilgrims look after one another, but if this sounds claustrophobic to you, consider staying at one or two *albergues* and patch in a hotel or two. The price goes up certainly, and you'll be on your own for meals, but the solitude of having a room with a door that closes and a bath you don't share might be the thing that keeps you going.

There's no wrong way to do this! Remind yourself it's the one chance in your life when you can get what you need. You need to make some friends and share your experiences? Go check into the *albergue*. You need solitude, don't want to talk, need some time for reflection or prayers where you are not also walking, then go check into a hotel or a *pensión* – and make no apologies. In fact, pilgrims with more financial resources might want to do this more often so that the cheaper accommodations go to the less financially endowed pilgrims. One of the biggest complaints is when wealthy pilgrims fill up the cheaper *albergues*, leaving the pricier places to the ones who can least afford them.

On a funny note, I planned to check into a hotel in a small town near the beginning of the *Camino Francés* with my daughter a few years ago. When we got to the front desk, leaving our walking companions to forage ahead for an inexpensive municipal *albergue*, we found a sign saying there was an *albergue* right there, inside the hotel. We were shown a private room with private bath and laundry facilities down the hall on the lower floor of the hotel. We were able to get a nice breakfast without having to leave the place. When we caught up with our friends from the day before, they made some snide comments about our staying in the fancy hotel – until we told them we paid just about what they had.

On the opposite end of this spectrum, you can in fact book accommodations every night as a way to ensure you have someplace to stay that you can count on at every stage. The caution is simply this: what do you do if you find that the next seven kilometers to your reservation is just too much to walk, and you are standing in front of a municipal *albergue* where everyone looks happy and cared for? This one day can throw all of your reservations off-balance and you will find yourself walking to accommodate your past self and not appreciating how this walk has changed you. The changes might be slight, but they are real.

Consider what it would be like just to walk, just turn to the left as you walk out the door in the morning and walk until you are hungry or walk until you need to find someplace to sleep. All the while, you are motivated to get to your goal: the Cathedral in Santiago de Compostela. It's quite liberating and the sense of accomplishment when you have navigated a whole day on your own like this is quite real and it can be quite profound.

It's also an amazing experience to realize how little you really need in a day. Something to eat, some water, a couple of bathroom breaks (especially if you aren't comfortable making use of the side of the road), and a place to rest.

And while there is certainly routine to all of this walking, each day will bring you something new, something challenging, something fun. Or something scary! And the sum total of these small events will be what you remember. You rise, eat, walk, eat, arrive, wash up, rest, eat, and sleep. That's it. Leave the baggage at home. Appreciate your surroundings, acknowledge your skills.

Breathe. It's all good. And remember, there is no more satisfying realization than this: "I did it!"

Planning Days of Walking

This can become the trickiest part of getting into your walk. If you have the funds and can afford one-way plane tickets or open-ended return flights, you might want to travel like that. It would fix the date of departure, for instance, to July 1 (arriving July 2 if you fly into Spain from outside Western Europe, walking starting July 3). Then you just walk until you arrive in Santiago, maybe spend a few days there – it's a wonderful town – and return when you are ready to leave, not on a fixed return date.

If you need to purchase round trip tickets, allow for a couple of days' rest *en route* and a couple of days at the end to decompress and explore Santiago de Compostela. I recommend that very strongly. Throwing yourself back into your routine right away is never the best way to come off walking the *Camino*. For mental health as well as physical health, take a day or two after your pilgrimage to lie around and visit the Cathedral museum, have a drink at a café, enjoy some *tapas*, and take a nap!

You should also know that you do not need to walk an entire *camino*. What I mean is this: you can break up the entire route into segments that may fit your work schedule or school schedule better than taking a six-week break to do the entire *Camino Francés*.

If you only have a week, you might walk from Sarria. If you have two weeks, you might start in O'Cebreiro, three weeks, León, four weeks, and so on. Or you may start walking in St. Jean Pied de Port or Pamplona and stop when you run out of days off, picking up the trail on your next trip from where you stop this time. I've done that. I have back to back stamps on my *credencial* from the Burgos Cathedral – one from when I stopped in 2014, one again when I started walking again in 2016.

In other words, make this what you need. Don't let anyone tell you how, when, or where to walk the *Camino*. It's meant to be a journey of the self, a journey for you, a journey to get closer to you and what you need.

What Will This Cost?

If you buy breakfast at a bar, as of this writing, the standard fare can run between three and five euros. That's for toast, fresh juice, and a large coffee with milk, a *café con leche*. If you're not crazy about drinking lots of milk with your breakfast, try a *cortado*. It's still the espresso you're looking for, but with only a splash of milk.

Lunch can be a hearty local soup, a sandwich of ham and cheese, or a Spanish *tortilla* – a standard omelet made with potatoes and sometimes onions or ham. If you pass through a town mid-day, you might find a *Menú del Día* or *Menú del Peregrino* with three courses for 10-12 euros at a restaurant or bar.

Albergues typically cost under 10 euros a night for a bunk bed, shared bathroom facilities, and frequently, either a place to cook your meal for dinner or a communal meal served by the *hospitaleros* or your fellow pilgrims. *Pensiónes* can run 30-45 euros, and hotels upwards from 45 euros.

Put simply – in addition to the immense spiritual benefits of a walking pilgrimage, this is by far the least expensive way to enjoy Spain. You can certainly spend more while you are walking, but it's definitely not necessary.

If you are walking in what we might call high season, i.e. over the summer, you should consider making some reservations at private *albergues* or *pensiónes.* It's always the least expensive places that fill up first and a certain number of pilgrims will want only to spend the night in *albergues*, thinking this is the only true pilgrimage experience. Please remember to make this walk what you need and if you need fresh towels you don't have to use, dry, and carry, by all means, check into a nice little *pensión* and get a good night's rest. You will be supporting the local economy and that's never a bad thing.

Can I Do This?

I'd say, yes, yes you can. Some pilgrims will insist on training for months by circumnavigating a local park, walking to the grocery store, getting off the bus one stop early – all well and good. But there's also nothing wrong with just buying plane tickets and walking out the door. If you decide on the popular *Camino Francés*, you will find there are bars and restaurants, shops and *albergues* all along the route so you can stop for a little rest every few kilometers in many sections of the *Camino*. You do need to be able to walk and your abilities and motivation will be tested, but do you need to be a ninja warrior? Most definitely, no. Many pilgrims have retired and are walking the *Camino* because unlike the rest of us, they don't have day jobs to scurry back to.

Plan this one out. It's not like a vacation trip. Allow yourself a day to get acclimated and a day or two to unwind. Give yourself the gift of a day off – or two! – so you can explore a lovely town or take in some wonderful scenery. Unlike lots of trips where you spend most of the day looking after everyone but yourself, this one is different. You will be looking out for yourself in ways you may not be used to – how do I feel, how do my knees feel, do I need to set down my pack, do I need to get something to drink other than water, is it time to get something to eat, do I need to sit down for a few minutes?

The key to great walking is looking after yourself – your physical health is important. Many days can make you feel like you are suddenly a part of an unannounced endurance test. But it doesn't mean you won't get something out of even the most challenging days.

Let's Get Started!

Nervous? Apprehensive? Excited? That's all normal. You are setting out on an adventure.

The clothes you wear may be unfamiliar to you, the shoes, the terrain, and the destination – all of these things may be new. The trick is to prepare and to ask for help from one of the following sources.

The Camino Forum: One of the very best, certainly one of the most comprehensive of these sources, is the Camino Forum, run in Casa Ivar in Santiago de Compostela by Ivar Rekve. Become a member and read the posts (see the postscript for a list of helpful website locations, publications, and resources). Pilgrims will answer first-time pilgrims' questions. Reading previous threads of conversations is tremendously helpful: you'll find advice on the best places to stay in any given town, or the best time of year to walk, is it safe to travel alone (yes!), what resources will I have access to if I lose my medications, my contacts, my way! Each of the various routes have their own section and their regular Forum followers. Log in, ask a question if you don't already see the answer, and expect a dozen replies in the next hour.

The American Pilgrims on the Camino (APOC): this is the central, organizing group for pilgrims in the United States. There are many local chapters, like my home chapter in New York City, and there is a core group of volunteers who run yearly "Gatherings" and U.S.-based *hospitalero* training.

The Confraternity of St. James: This group publishes the most wonderful and always reliable guide books – and they are updated frequently. They are the largest and oldest English-speaking pilgrims' association. The Confraternity guides, which you can buy on their website, will tell you when to call ahead, when to avoid certain sections of the routes if the weather is not good, how many beds are available in each *albergue*, and in many cases, how to get to Mass – not always the easiest task to accomplish, given that so many of Spain's churches are not staffed with their own priests but rather share priests who say Mass in more than one location.

Gronze is another important website that is very popular in Spain. Each of the routes is laid out in stages with helpful information on the options for places to stay. It is really comprehensive but there is a note of caution: while there are many, many ways to get to the Cathedral from many points in Spain, not all of them are approved by the Cathedral as bonafide *caminos*. The routes which are acceptable pilgrimage routes are listed on the Cathedral website (resource in my postscript).

Camino Tour Operators: Surprisingly, some of the best itineraries can be planned by cribbing the Spanish tour operators' tour plans. If they offer a 10-day walking tour, say, starting in the beautiful mountain town of O'Cebreiro, you can get a sense of how many kilometers they plan to walk every day, where their group will stay, what sights they will take in, and then you can decide either to sign up and go along with them or take the information, stash it in your planning folder (yes, you really should make one of these), and make use of their expertise.

Apps: Everyone has their favorite, but mine is called Eroski Consumer Camino. It's written in Spanish, but the vocabulary will recur and it gets easier to understand every time you use it. This one app might be all you need if you intend to plan the route yourself and stay in *albergues*. All the major routes are covered. You'll find the number of beds available in each *albergue*, whether or not they offer clothes washing services or washing machines for pilgrims to use, whether or not you will be offered a meal in the evening and breakfast the next day, and the going rate for a bed. And there is a brilliant elevation map so you can see where you'll be climbing and where the trail is flat. You even get a little photo of each *albergue* so you'll know it when you see it. It seems like a little thing, I suppose, but I find it tremendously comforting to spot my *albergue* in the distance after walking for hours to get there.

Wise Pilgrim: These guides are widely used as well. I used both the *Camino Primitivo* and the *Camino Inglés* guides and found the narrative to be extremely helpful. WP got me right out of Oviedo the day I started

– it's a challenging start through a fairly large urban area. Many pilgrims that I met who stopped for the night in Grado, where I worked as a volunteer, told stories of wandering around Oviedo, not finding anything helpful to get them out of town and on their journey. I hoped they would pick up the app at least, going forward. WP also sells a beautiful poster with all of the *caminos* charted out on a map of Spain – so you can plot out your next walk!

John Brierley: If there is a "Grand Old Man" of the *Camino*, it would have to be John Brierley – and he's not that old either! Nearly every English-speaking pilgrim will carry one of his books. They offer colorful maps, detailed information of places to stay – including hotels – and lovely reflections on how the route might feed your soul. I have found that the Brierley guides are better during the core season (mid-March through early October) than they are for "off" season (after late October to early March). The book will lead you to stop in places that may close in the winter months.

Best advice? Get to all of these resources and see what you can make work for you. Then, get out and buy a compass! My little compass saved me many times midday when the sun was directly overhead and I had convinced myself I couldn't find my way west.

Last note: get the **Rome2rio** app. It's not *Camino*-specific, it's about travel from place to place. A French pilgrim who stopped at the albergue where I was volunteering needed just to go home right away. The first thing we asked her was, "Do you have **Rome2rio**?" She wanted to go from Grado in Asturias on the *Camino Primitivo* to the south of France. It took just a few seconds to plan her route.

Random Tips

Avoiding blisters – after you've resolved the socks issue and you feel pretty comfortable in your boots, let me recommend you tape up your feet. It's what many dancers do. You stretch and stick paper tape across key contact points on your feet. You'll get pretty close to eliminating the chance you'll get blisters. It's not 100% effective or guaranteed, but from my experience, it gets the job done.

Make sure your feet are clean, then put strips of tape around the back of your heels, along the side of your feet and across your toes. Then, if you still get blisters, open them, drain them, clean them, apply some Neosporin or some Chapstick along with a nice big Band-Aid and more paper tape and you will be good to go.

The many ways to both prevent and cure blisters are argued by pretty much everybody I know. I met a woman who insisted slathering her feet with Vaseline was what kept her from getting blisters. And others recommend deer tallow cream (Hirschtalg Creme) which

I do not believe is sold in the U.S. I'm completely grossed out by the idea of slip-sliding my way into my socks with Vaseline all over my feet so I stick with my paper tape to protect my tootsies from my boots. I own Hirschtalg Creme but I could not talk myself into using it. This is just another one of those personal decisions. If it works for you, don't listen to me!

Finding your boots – once you arrive at an *albergue*, you will be asked to remove your boots and leave your hiking poles inside the door, not bringing them into the dormitory. I have seen the horrified look of someone who had another pilgrim mistakenly pick up her boots. It's not something you ever want to happen to you. People don't steal boots here, but so many people wear similar styles and colors, it's easy enough to pick up the wrong boots – or to leave your poles in the *albergue* and set out without them.

I use 8" yellow, coated wires to identify my boots and poles. I have two of them – one that slips through the tabs on my boots, and one that goes through the hand grips on my poles. That way, I can see right away which are mine and it reminds me that since I have two wires, I grab up my poles as well. The wires were purchased at the Container Store. They are meant to keep computer cables together.

You can use pink or turquoise shoelaces, strips of plaid ribbon – anything that will identify your boots as yours. It will be so easy getting out in the morning if you don't have to search for your boots from among a dozen pairs that look a lot like yours.

On the *Camino*, you will see many places that offer a pilgrim's menu (*Menú del Peregrino* in Spanish). What that means is a three-course meal with wine and tap water and it's very reasonably priced, but it is a lot of food. When I walk, I do not have much of an appetite and I feel guilty leaving food that I don't want to carry with me the next day, so I found a way around it. I order one of the pieces of the *menú*, but not all of the *menú*. That way, I can get the spaghetti with meat sauce but don't have to commit to a second course of chicken with potatoes followed by dessert if all I really want is that spaghetti. For some reason, on my 2017 *Camino*, I craved spaghetti and had it in a lot of places. I was happy both to find a solution to the *menú* guilt and to save a few euros not buying the whole *menú.*

Famously, I sat down at one *albergue* with an adjoining restaurant and asked if the kitchen could just scramble me a couple of eggs. That was all I wanted. The waitress brought me three perfectly scrambled eggs that I had with some fresh bread and a hot tea. It was just what I needed. But I left, thinking they would add the bill to my tab and I was planning to pay in the morning. When I came down to the bar to get breakfast, I mentioned that I had not paid for dinner yet. The cook said, "No worries. We all remember you. You didn't eat enough to pay for dinner. It's on the house."

And you can, in many places, share a *menú.* Check with the waiter. You can order two servings of the first course and get fruit to share for dessert, or order one first and one second course. It will cost a few euro more than eating it by yourself, but if you are with someone who is also not that hungry, it's the perfect solution.

Many towns will offer vegetarian options, either in the grocery stores or the restaurants and cafes and the *hospitalero* will be able to get you information or maps so you can find what you need easily. One particular *albergue* is highly recommended: Albergue Verde in Hospital de Órbigo offers food they grow in their own garden and they are very accommodating to pilgrims with dietary restrictions or food allergies.

There's not much difference between the two *menús*, *Menú del Día* or *Menú del Peregrino*, but you should always identify yourself as a pilgrim so you have a chance of being served food in the evening before the restaurant opens for dinner – typically 8:30 p.m. This can be an issue for Americans who are used to eating dinner between 6:00 p.m. and 7:00 p.m. And since most *albergues* close between 9:30 p.m. and 10:00 p.m., you want not to be rushed while eating. Keep in mind though, if you spend time in Madrid after your walk, dinner gets going there closer to midnight.

One caveat: if you are served a croissant with a fork, use the fork. The sugary glaze coating will glue up your fingers. It's not pretty. Tasty, but messy.

Drinks — when you stop at a bar while walking, consider trying something other than one more coffee. I like to swap in a hot green tea, or an Aquarius. Aquarius comes in two flavors – orange and lemon. It's a non-fizzy kind of lemonade or orangeade that is close to Gatorade and it will refresh you but not leave you with a sticky sweet aftertaste the way many soda drinks will. But then, there's really something wonderful about knocking back an ice-cold Coke after a long day. I'm not a beer drinker, but Spain offers several popular beers and beer drinks. And if you crave a *Sangría* but want to save a few euro, order a *Tinto de Verano* – what I call a "Poor Man's *Sangría*." It's just a glass of red wine with a splash of Fanta or *La Casera*, a Spanish fizz drink. Like a red wine spritzer. I get the Fanta – *limón* flavor.

Bi-Frutas — one of my favorite things to carry. *Bi-Frutas* is a multi-fruit drink that comes in little cardboard drink boxes in a couple of flavors, and six boxes will run you about a euro. They will make the difference when you are walking and need something to drink other than water. They can add a few calories and you can toss the little box at the next place you stop.

Journals – do you need to write down everything that happens to you while you are walking? Maybe you do. I'm a lousy journal writer myself. I tend to just write down sad little comments about what I eat because I don't have much to say in the moment. I'm more likely to write about it later. However, this is a personal choice. Many people keep diaries or blogs that they publish while walking. It can be a way to share what you are doing — or it can become a distraction, once you have followers who need to know each day what you are doing. I met a young girl, a student, who decided it was easier to direct everyone to her blog than to re-tell the same stories over and over to her family and her friends. But social media being what it is, I could see where she could spend some significant time every day logging in and writing her travelogue instead of staying present in the moment and checking in later, after she finished walking.

One of the things you might want to write about are the kindnesses of the people you meet along the *Camino*. Pick up enough Spanish before you leave with an app or a course to allow yourself the opportunity to speak with local residents of the towns and villages you pass through. It can become the highlight of your pilgrimage.

You want to be able to talk to people, especially if you need something or want to learn more about your surroundings. I asked for help finding a nice place for lunch in Melide. I was walking through and, because I knew Melide well enough from working nearby in Ribadiso and walking through twice on pilgrimage, I could see I was just about out of town and hadn't found a good place to eat. So, I asked an older woman for assistance. She said she was on her way to the cemetery but would be glad to find me a nice lunch and did I need an *albergue* as well? I reassured her that all I wanted was lunch and she walked me down a slender alleyway that opened out to a large area with many restaurants and bars – which I never would have seen on my own.

I walked across a farm on my way to Castello on the *Camino Primitivo*. The path I was on passed directly in front of a house where five older people were chatting. As I walked by, the man on the end nodded toward the bench next to him, indicating that I should come over and sit for a moment to rest. I did and he asked me where I was from. "New York," I said. And where did you grow up, he asked. "Michigan, sir." He then went on to name all the states' names he knew, commenting on the political climate, and whether it might rain later. Then, he pointed his finger right at me and asked, "Do you believe in the Saint, or are you just walking?"

I assured him that I believed in the Saint and that, in fact, I believed that the Saint guides my feet every day. I took a quick selfie with him and his companion on the bench and went back to walking.

In my several times walking the *Camino*, I've been offered a few pieces of hard candy from a man whose house we walked by, fresh fruit, *tapas*, desserts, cheese from a couple having dinner near me at a restaurant – many people will want to become a brief part of your pilgrimage. A woman from Ireland offered to carry my backpack up a hill. A young man from California asked if I needed water. Another couple asked if I wanted some dried fruit.

Sometimes you may receive a kindness by someone you never see. I stopped to refill my pocket water bottle with water from my spare. It was hot that day and I was being cautious. As I took off my backpack and set it alongside the road, a car passed me. I didn't notice really until I looked up and saw they had stopped about 75 meters ahead of me. They were waiting to see if I was alright. How did I know this? Because as soon as I picked up my pack to start walking again, they drove away.

But the most curious of all offers was from the walnut man and his wife. I was walking somewhere in Galicia with my two daughters when a man and his wife come up to us and offered us each a single walnut. Not really knowing what to do with this lovely gesture, we all nodded and mumbled something at which he then said, "Please. Take these to Santiago for me." Which we did, of course. We left them on the fountain near the entrance to the Cathedral. Since then, every time I tell that story to my fellow pilgrims, they all say, "I met him, too!"

Sign your *credencial!* At least make sure your name is on it. That way, when you leave it at the *albergue* by mistake or it falls out of the side pocket on your backpack, someone will be able to get it to you. While I cannot recommend you leave anything at an *albergue* when you get out in the morning, at least if your name is on it, you have a good chance of getting it back. And when you arrive at the Pilgrims' Office, it will make it easier to process your paperwork if your name is on the *credencial.* If you get yours from APOC, it will have your name typed in it already. A great solution!

As you leave your overnight place to start walking in the morning, no matter where you stay, make sure you have your cellphone in your hand as you walk out the door. You do not want to walk all day without it, arrive at the day's destination, hire a cab, and go back to the previous town, all because you walked out the door without the phone in your hand. That's not fun.

If your backpack starts to slow you down and you've lightened your load as much as you can, there are what are called "*Mochila* Transports." This is a service run locally in several locations along the road that will pick up your backpack (*mochila* in Spanish) at the place where you've spent the night and take it to the next town for you. That way, you can walk all day without carrying it. I've used this service several times and, in each case, it was a great decision. It's not an expensive proposition. Five to ten euros, give or take, will get your bag from where you are now to where you will be by the end of the day.

Just a few caveats to *mochila* transport – one is that there are *albergues* which will not accept or send backpacks for any reason. You may also find municipal *albergues* which will not check you in if you are not carrying your backpack. These are few, but they are there. And if you send your bag forward to a hotel, be sure to keep the name of your hotel on you so you can meet up with your bag with no issues. I met a woman a few years ago who had sent her bag ahead WITH the reservation information and the location of her hotel inside the bag. She could not remember which transport service she had used or where her bag went!

Correos (the Spanish postal service) is the latest to get into this backpack business. It was a logical next step for the local post offices since they already had the infrastructure in place to move packages – or backpacks – between cities along the *Camino* in Spain. It's called *Camino con Correos.*

But, is it cash or credit? The simple answer is, "Yes." Bring cash enough to last you a week or so and a Visa debit/credit card to get you more cash from a bank ATM for the next week. While you can use American debit/credit cards along the *Camino* in larger cities to pay for transportation (trains or buses) or hotels, cash will be necessary everywhere else. *Albergues*, *pensiones*, and bars in villages and small towns will be cash only, and the handful of large shops that do accept card payments will be Visa cards only. Be sure to notify your bank at home that you will be traveling so they don't think your charges and ATM withdrawals in Spain are fraudulent. It's just a phone call – but it's important! Then, be careful using an American card in airport shops. That's the only place we've had trouble with someone appropriating our credit card number.

Arriving in Santiago de Compostela

And now you're here. This is a day that will bring you a roller coaster of emotions: you'll start with the thrill of seeing the Cathedral and the other arriving pilgrims and then feel like you've suddenly lost a good friend when you realize you won't be walking again tomorrow. It's good to take a minute to experience all of this, because it won't last.

You should start by dropping off your backpack at your hotel, *albergue*, or *pensión*. I like to make reservations for this day so I know where I'm going and can make better time getting into the Cathedral. I can recommend three places that I have stayed that are very centrally located and are really nice to exhausted pilgrims – the Pensión Hortas, Hotel San Francisco, and the Hotel Rua Villar where I have stayed so many times they recognize me when I check in. Get a shower, change your boots, and get over to the Cathedral to pay your respects to the Saint.

I recommend you bring only what you need and enjoy the fact that you are now walking without that backpack. Take your passport, your *credencial*, and some cash. You will not be able to enter with your hiking backpack, so I always recommend leaving it at your place for the night, before coming to the Cathedral.

You will enter the Cathedral not through the central doors that face the main square (Plaza Obradoiro) but on the south side, up the stairs from the fountain (Plaza de Platerías). That's where we left those walnuts.

Once inside you will be in the transept and the main altar will be in front of you but facing to your left. You will see a roped area alongside the main altar where you will be able to embrace the Saint. There is a slim staircase that goes up to a metal and jewel-encrusted bust of Saint James. He overlooks the main altar, facing into the nave, or central body of the church. You will step up behind the bust and embrace it. It's part of the traditional set of protocols for arriving pilgrims.

Down the other side, you'll see another queue and a small doorway that leads to the crypt where you will find the silver reliquary that houses the remains of the Saint. You can kneel there to say a quick prayer or light a candle directly behind the kneeler, then walk back up the other side and out into the ambulatory that will take you into the main body of the church.

Next stop?

Get your *Compostela!* You've earned it.

The Pilgrims' Office is on a side street not adjacent to the Cathedral. You reach it by walking back out to the main square in front of the Cathedral (on the west side of the building) and across the front of the grand hotel Hostal dos Reis Católicos, located just to the left as you face the former main entrance to the church. Pass along the front of the hotel, keep left, and then down the stone ramp until you reach the street (Rúa Carretas) – a sharp right turn, then walk to the end of this block, just past the small Correos office. In addition to *mochila* transport, you can also use them to ship things home if you decide to keep walking or have other plans in Europe that do not include your hiking gear.

I like to send my big water bottle, my hiking poles and my travel quilt or sleeping bag home via

Correos to keep extra space in my pack and avoid the risk of having an airline employee refuse to allow the poles onboard the plane in my carry-on luggage. I like to get them home safely regardless — and the airport in Santiago has gotten very strict about this. You will not be able to carry hiking poles in your carry-on luggage if you fly in or out of this airport.

Once you present your *credencial* to the security guard in the Pilgrims' Office, you will cross the entryway and enter a corridor that leads to the staff who will write your certificate. The guards will ask you not to take photos in that corridor. A staff member, who will be able to speak with you in English, will review your *credencial*, ask a few questions, and write your certificate with your name translated into Latin. You may also request a certificate of distance to commemorate the number of kilometers you walked and your starting point. The Office staff will also take your picture, if you ask them. Then, buy a small mailing tube so you can transport these precious pieces of paper home safely.

And you're done.

As you leave the Office, you'll start running into people you walked with, seeing faces from days earlier, and catching up with your new family of pilgrims as they explore – with you – the small streets, the cafes, and the dozens of souvenir shops in Santiago de Compostela. Even if you started this journey alone, you are not alone now.

If you need to keep walking, because on some level one never stops walking, consider walking on to Finisterre or Muxía – to the end of the earth as it was known in Saint James' day. It's another week or so walking – or a bus ride! – and the seafood is fabulous. It's a remarkable feeling to stand at the edge of the Atlantic – the opposite edge from my home in New York – knowing that it was only the sea that could stop walking pilgrims, as it did Saint James when he first came to Iberia to preach.

As a footnote: the shell you carry has its roots in the Middle Ages when pilgrims would bring home scallop shells to prove they'd been to the end of the earth. There are several elaborate and complicated shell legends. This is the one I like.

Now You're Home

First, you will miss the camaraderie of your fellow pilgrims. You will miss the coffee at breakfast that everyone takes for granted and you knew it was spectacular, and absolutely, you will miss Spain.

I also found that I needed to recreate the solitude I found by walking most of my *caminos* by myself. For me, it's found in empty churches. While I love seeing a full church, lit up to the rafters with candles and chandeliers, with the organ playing and people singing, I do love to slip in quietly to sit in the back of an empty church. I cherish a few moments in a sacred space.

I have a dear friend who told me once that the prayers that are voiced inside churches will stay there long after the prayerful have left. These entreaties to God or the saints are embedded in the walls, the floor, the benches, and they echo and reverberate even after everyone is gone, when the church is empty. That's what I keep looking for now.

If you think you might want to volunteer in some fashion with the *Camino*, there are several ways to get involved, while you plan how quickly you can go back.

You can join a local chapter of the pilgrim association. And if there is not a local chapter, you might think about starting one. Maybe you'd like to work in an *albergue*. APOC offers *hospitalero* training as do most other pilgrims' associations. This training, over several days, will give you an idea of what it would be like to look after pilgrims and would identify you to the Spanish Federation, so you could apply for an official volunteer assignment. It sounds more complicated than it is. After just a few days in training, you will be able to apply to a post in Spain by identifying the fifteen days you would like to work and where you would like to be assigned. Get in touch with APOC when you return to get information on how to get to their training. You may be offered a post near the place you liked while you were walking or you could find yourself in a place you don't know at all – which can be really wonderful. I've done both.

You can also research *albergues* on Facebook, certainly, and Eroski which features a section with pilgrim-written reviews. Get a sense of their way of doing things, look at photos, and then write to the *albergue* directly to offer your services. I've done that, too.

In either event, training is essential. *Hospitaleros* on the *Camino* are trained to protect pilgrims in a very special way. It requires a skill set that's a combination of soccer coach, parenting, and working as a mental health professional to be able to listen to the stories all day and be able to find what your pilgrims need during their stay with you. The walking can be refreshing, of course, but sometimes, it can also be stressful. I have discovered that a solid night's rest will recharge me every time for another day of walking, but I do like to talk to the *hospitaleros*. And I love it if they know how to listen.

The nice people who write *Compostelas* can also be volunteers. There is a regular staff but they are augmented by scores of pilgrim volunteers. If you have a particular gift with languages, this might be the job for you. Application to these posts is made directly to the Office.

And how will you know it's time to walk again? Many people swear right away, "I will never do this again!" But I tell people it's simple to know when you are ready to start planning another walk. You will be shopping for a shirt. You'll find your size and the color you were looking for, but before you check out, you ask yourself, "Gee, I wonder what it weighs."

That's when you know.

Walking the equivalence of the entire length of Manhattan every day for a month is not for everyone. And you might think you just could never make it. But we do. We get up, we buy plane tickets, and we go. We learn about ourselves and the planet in a way that I cannot find anywhere else. We make lifelong friends from all over the world. And sometimes, the smallest thing will make the biggest impact.

When my father was seriously ill, I called my youngest daughter and asked her to bring me some clothes when she flew out to Michigan to be with us. I told her I really needed a "shawl." But she misheard me. When she arrived, she handed me a "shell" from the *Camino*, one of the ones I had carried on my backpack. Even though I thought I needed a wrap to keep me warm, she knew on another level, inherently because she too is a pilgrim, that the shell was what I was really asking for.

Buen Camino, pilgrim. May your walk be easy and your rewards great.

Dear American Pilgrim

I was so nervous embarking on my first walk, so I can imagine you might be as well. Even veteran hikers – which I most definitely am not! – will find this hike unlike others you may have taken. The challenges you face may be of your own making: you've brought too much stuff. Or they may be weather-related, or they may be related to the reason you decide to walk. But they are all a part of this. Pilgrims do leave home, they take a leap of faith, and they accomplish great big things.

Please don't feel like you are merely attending a local cultural event in another country, like the Palio in Siena or Mardi Gras in Rio where you might watch but not participate. This is for you. This is for anyone who needs it. It's been likened to the creation of the European Union – that it's a way for many cultural traditions to meet in one place for shared goals and common ambitions.

I've prepared this little book for you with much love. It's filled with lots of information I wish I had before I walked. I want you to feel secure, I want you to be able to anticipate things that will happen along the way. And when you get where you're going, I want you to be comfortable and confident performing the simple pilgrim protocols all pilgrims perform.

One last little story: when I arrived at the Cathedral in 2010, in the middle of the craziness of their closing the Holy Door for the year and after walking by myself, I had no idea what I was supposed to do. I followed the crowd and found my way in through the Door, to the embrace of the Saint, and down the stairs for the veneration in the crypt, but I missed something that I cannot now do again: touching the *trumeau* in the medieval *Portico de la Gloria*. The *trumeau* is the slender support column between the two arched doorway openings into the Cathedral inside the west façade. Pilgrims used to enter the church building there and place their open hand along the right-hand side of the *trumeau*. You can see Martin Sheen doing this in the movie, "The Way," which was filmed in 2009 when that was still possible.

Since 2009, much restoration work has been done on that doorway and now, you will need to make arrangements with the Cathedral Museum to see it. In the beginning of the work, the west door was still open and the work went on around it, but over time, it meant closing that entrance altogether and rerouting people to the south entrance where it's likely you will enter the Cathedral now. The repeated touching of that column by more than 800 years' worth of grateful, arriving pilgrims was jeopardizing the future of the stonework. In 2010, as you walked in the grand front entrance doors, you could place your hand in the impression made by all of those hands. Now, no. But I didn't know I was supposed to do it.

This route has been walked by saints and kings, by popes and movie stars. Shirley McLaine wrote a popular book about it. Suze Orman walked a few years ago. Keep your wits about you, but please do not be afraid. You can do this – and you can let me know how it goes. I'm at tweedpilgrim@gmail.com, if you need me.

Buen Camino!

We don't think about pilgrimage in this country. We don't think about meditation. The idea of taking a six-week walk is totally foreign to most Americans. But it's probably exactly what we need.

• Emilio Estevez

Glossary

Albergue – pronounced Owl-Bear-Gay with the emphasis on the Bear. This is the Spanish word for the pilgrim hostels along the *Camino*. They are typically large municipal buildings of several stories with a large central room on the ground floor and a dormitory or set of dormitories on the upper floor or floors. They are staffed typically by volunteers but may also have a professional staff that is responsible for checking in pilgrims as they arrive and keeping the place clean. Private *albergues* are owned by individuals who may also reserve beds in advance for arriving pilgrims. They tend to be a few euros more expensive than the municipal *albergues* and charge a fixed fee.

Casa Rural – unlike *albergues* which tend to be in town or right close to town, a *casa rural* can be out in the countryside. Typically, they are renovated antique country homes with unique elements, like gourmet cooking, terraces, and patios. You will also see *pazos* on the *Camino Portugués*. They are Galician manor houses turned into luxury accommodations. Some with their own vineyards. Both are privately owned.

Compostela – the official document, written in Latin, that is presented to arriving pilgrims in Santiago de Compostela to affirm that the pilgrim has successfully completed their pilgrimage and has walked at minimum the last 100 kilometers to the Cathedral.

Credencial – your pilgrim passport. This is a folded paper document that is available from the Cathedral, pilgrim associations around the world, *albergues*, and churches along the *Camino*. Pilgrims carry this passport for two key reasons: one, to be allowed entry into *albergues* and two, to collect rubber stamp impressions in order to qualify for the *Compostela*. Each of these stamps identifies the place where you receive it. Two stamps each day while you walk the last 100 kilometers are required to qualify for the *Compostela*. It was recommended to me in Ferrol that the stamps be from a minimum of two different locations each day, i.e. not just two in the same town.

Donativo – an *albergue* paid by donation. *Albergues* that are called *donativos* will house you for a donation rather than a published fee. This does not mean you can elect not to pay anything. It means you can decide how much to offer your hosts for their hospitality.

Hospitalera/o – the lovely people who look after you at *albergues* along the routes. They are trained, professional, mostly volunteers, mostly former pilgrims.

Menú del Peregrino – a three-course meal served at a fixed price at many restaurants for lunch and/or dinner. Typically, you will be served earlier in the evening if you identify yourself as a pilgrim. Most Spain restaurants do not start serving dinner until 8:30 p.m.

Mochila Transport – local services that will collect your backpack and drop it off at the next stop. The fees vary but overall, this is a relatively inexpensive operation.

You'll find slips when you check into the *albergue*, if that *albergue* offers a pick-up service to pilgrims – not all do. You fill out the slip and leave it in the common area or at a designated spot with the fee. Be sure to contact the carrier to make sure they pick it up – especially if you are in smaller or less popular locations.

Best is to keep a day pack with you for your really important items: passport, *credencial*, wallet or change purse, snacks, any medications, and water. You can expect to see your backpack again at the next town, either at a designated drop-off spot, like a local bar or the Correos office if you use their *Paq Mochila* service, or at the place you identify to the service, sometimes a hotel or *pensión*, sometimes the next *albergue*.

Resources

I recommend just what I have used again and again and found helpful. There are nearly as many resources for pilgrims now as there are pilgrims.

- Websites
  - American Pilgrims on the Camino
    www.americanpilgrims.org/
  - Camino Forum
    www.caminodesantiago.me/
  - Catedral de Santiago de Compostela
    www.catedraldesantiago.es/
  - Confraternity of St. James
    www.csj.org.uk/
  - Eroski
    www.caminodesantiago.consumer.es/
  - Gronze
    www.gronze.com/
  - Rome2rio.com
  - Wise Pilgrim
    www.wisepilgrim.com

🐚 Books

- o Jean-Christie Ashmore: "Camino de Santiago: To Walk Far, Carry Less," Walk Far Media, 2011

- o John Brierley: "A Pilgrim's Guide to the Camino de Santiago," Camino Guides, 2017

- o David Downie: "Paris to the Pyrenees: A Skeptic Pilgrim Walks the Way of Saint James," Pegasus Books, 2014

- o Johnnie Walker: "It's About Time," Redemptorist Pastoral Publications, 2019

- o David Whitson and Laura Perazzoli: "The Northern Caminos: Norte, Primitivo and Inglés," Cicerone Guides, 2015

- o David Whyte: "Pilgrim," Many Rivers Press, 2012

N.B. The Confraternity of St. James guidebooks are all helpful. Up to date, thoroughly researched, lovingly presented. Very highly recommended. Available on their website.

Apps for your Smartphone

- o Camino Forum
- o Eroski Consumer Camino
- o Rome2rio
- o Wise Pilgrim

American Movies

- o "The Way," Elixir Films, 2010. It stars Martin Sheen, playing an eye doctor from California, and Emilio Estevez, who plays his adult son.
- o "The Camino Documentary: Six Ways to Santiago," Virgil Films & Entertainment, 2013. American filmmaker Lydia Smith follows six pilgrims as they walk.
- o "Strangers on the Earth," Walk to Fisterra, 2018. An American cellist carries his cello across the *Camino Frances* to Finisterre.

My photos: Redbubble.com/people/nilesite

My blog: TumbleweedPilgrim.com

Look for the next Tumbleweed Pilgrim guide for
pilgrims – to the Cathedral of Santiago de Compostela
(Fall 2020)

Postscript – on "Booking Ahead"

In the movie, "The Way," there is an awful argument between two characters about what makes for a true pilgrim. Do they beg from strangers, live off the land, look for handouts all along the road, and take what the day dishes out, or do they use credit cards, stay in hotels, eat in restaurants, and enjoy themselves while they walk? I have a sneaking suspicion that if I were to come up to the road and confront a pilgrim in the 13th century, walking to the new Cathedral in Santiago de Compostela, and offer them a room with a private shower, towels, blankets, and a hot meal for a few *reales*, they would probably take me up on that offer.

So, how do you square away your wanting to be true with your needing some creature comforts and reassurances?

With the increase in the number of pilgrims walking to Santiago these days, there is a semi-valid reason to worry about where you'll spend the night, especially if you select the summer months for your walk. I say "semi" because I worked in an *albergue* during July 2019 and we were only filled (with 62 beds) two or three times in the fifteen days I was there, on the most crowded section of the most popular route. Why? Everyone had booked ahead. I'd wave, they'd smile, and they'd shout to me, "We booked ahead!" And they would pass up a beautiful, half empty *albergue* for 6 Euros a night to stay at a small hotel or *pension* up the road a bit for 30-50 Euros.

They had read in the forums online that there was a bed crush, that folks were squeezed out of their ideal true pilgrim *albergue* experience, and if you arrived at the day's stopping point after noon or one o'clock, all beds would have been snapped up by pilgrims who left well before sunrise that morning, sometimes as early as 4:00 a.m. And let's be honest: all the guidebooks do send all the pilgrims to the same towns each day. Even with a fairly robust infrastructure, it can get crowded.

I can speak to this topic better now than before because since I started walking the various stages of the *Camino* over ten years ago, I now have had the experience of not only booking ahead but booking a self-guided tour from a *Camino* tour operator.

This is the question: can you be anything like a true pilgrim if you send your bags ahead with *mochila* transport, stay in hotels with reservations instead of walk-in *albergues*, taxi to and from your accommodations, and have the luxury of knowing where you are going to spend the night every day you walk? I think, yes.

I learned something really valuable when I walked the *Camino Ingles* in 2018. We walked early in the season, we saw next to no one walking every day, and we stayed in *albergues* every night but one – where there was no albergue in the town. Because the *Inglés* route is significantly less popular year 'round, we never had to worry about a place to stay. And because we didn't worry, we took our time. We lollygagged. We sauntered. We lay down in the grass and watched the clouds go by. We took advantage of local restaurants, visited churches and historic locations, had leisurely lunches, and enjoyed the whole adventure immensely. Why? Because, in the end, it is just about the walking and the getting there.

I am fortunate to know several *Camino* tour operators, any one of them offering very thoughtful excursions that will allow you to focus on the walking. The one my daughter and I took in April 2019 was just what we needed. Every day, we had a thorough itinerary with phone numbers of drivers if we needed help, with the directions to our hotels, and with notes about what not to miss along the way. We got up in the morning, left our bags with the front desk staff, had a late breakfast, got walking around 9 o'clock, stopped as needed, then called for transportation to that night's hotel. We would be taken back to where we left off the night before so we could continue walking – and all we had to do was walk.

Did this stop me from ever wanting to sleep in dormitories again, filled with snoring pilgrims in bunk beds? Oh, absolutely no. Now that I have done both, I can recommend both – as you need. I love seeing the *albergue* ahead of me at the end of a challenging day walking. But I can honestly say, having fluffy robes and towels was a treat.

How do you decide?

As long as the focus is on crafting this sacred journey into what you need, you will be a true pilgrim. It matters little where you spend the night. It can matter a great deal if you are not happy. Focus on the goal: to arrive safely in Santiago de Compostela and embrace the saint who helped get you there.

There were many stories this past summer (2019) of pilgrims reserving rooms and then not showing up. Have the courtesy to free up space for someone else if you decide to stop sooner or later than your reservation. But also realize, you have just added one more thing to your planning – where do I book, how does it fit into my budget, and how comfortable am I having a conversation in Spanish over the phone if I want to change or cancel my plan?

It is safe to say, that most of the places you book will be even more lovely than you imagined; run by families who have looked after pilgrims for generations.

One of my favorite small hotels is run by a woman who took over the business after her husband died. She redecorated with flowers everywhere. She runs the front desk while her daughter cleans and waits tables and the grandmother cooks in the hotel kitchen. If you spend the night in Grado on the *Camino Primitivo*, get in touch with me and I will give you the coordinates!

As we get closer to the Holy Year of 2021, there are mixed messages about crowds coming from my sources. Some people say it will have crushing crowds and everything will be filled months in advance. Others say it might be all hype and not any more crowded than summers are now. Regardless, if you do not know what walking in a Holy Year is like, please consider making some plans. Walking in 2010 from Sarria to Santiago de Compostela was unique among my walking experiences. There was a heightened sense that we were doing something particularly holy, that there was an added sacred quality to our walk that year. And I still remember the people I met: the young man on the bike who offered to carry my pack for me, the woman who was sitting by herself whispering prayers in the Cathedral, and the woman in the queue to walk through the Holy Door who kept my place for me while I checked my backpack. I arrived not realizing I couldn't bring my pack inside with me.

In the end, it is always the people you remember. Just like Suze Orman says: "People first." And when it comes to planning a pilgrimage – for the first time or just the next time – that means you first. Get what *you* need and make no apologies. "I need all *albergues*" or "I need all reservations" – both are valid, as long as the walk is what matters.

Remember the mantra: It's the walk and the getting there. We never judge our fellow pilgrims and we always thank St. James for guiding our feet.

From The Backpack Press

If you have enjoyed this book, please recommend it to your friends. If you would like to read more from Anne Born and The Backpack Press, try these, available on Amazon, Barnes & Noble, and by special order from your favorite independent bookseller.

A Marshmallow on the Bus

Prayer Beads on the Train

Waiting on a Platform

Turnstiles

Local Color

And from The Late Orphan Project:

These Winter Months

These Summer Months

Made in the USA
Middletown, DE
24 January 2022